What's On Your Plate?

Breakfast

Ted and Lola Schaefer

www.raintreepublishers.co.uk

Visit our website to find out more information about **Raintree** books.

To order:
☎ Phone 44 (0) 1865 888113
📄 Send a fax to 44 (0) 1865 314091
💻 Visit the Raintree bookshop at **www.raintreepublishers.co.uk**
to browse our catalogue and order online.

First published in Great Britain by Raintree, Halley Court, Jordan Hill, Oxford, OX2 8EJ, part of Harcourt Education.
Raintree is a registered trademark of Harcourt Education Ltd.

Editorial: Patrick Catel, Rosie Gordon and Melanie Waldron
Design: Phillipa Jenkins, Lucy Owen, John Walker
Picture Research: Melissa Allison
Production: Chloe Bloom

Originated by Chroma Graphics (Overseas) Pte Ltd.
Printed and bound in China by South China Printing Company

13-digit ISBN: 978 1 4062 0255 7
10-digit ISBN: 1 406 20255 X

10 09 08 07
10 9 8 7 6 5 4 3 2

British Library Cataloguing-in-Publication Data:

Schaefer, Lola M., 1950-
Breakfast. - (What's On Your Plate?)
1. Breakfasts - Juvenile literature 2. Natural foods - Juvenile literature 3. Nutrition - Juvenile literature
I. Title II. Schaefer, Ted, 1948-
641.3'02

A full catalogue record for this book is available from the British Library.

Acknowledgements

The publishers would like to thank the following for permission to reproduce photographs: **p. 29**, Corbis; **p. 17**, Corbis/Vince Streano; **p. 9**, Getty Images/Foodpix; **pp. 6, 26** Getty Images/Imagebank; **p. 4**, Getty Images/Photodisc; **pp. 10, 12, 14, 16, 19, 20, 21, 22, 23, 25, 27**, Harcourt Education Ltd/MM Studios; **pp. 15, 24, 28**, Harcourt Education Ltd/Tudor Photography; **p. 7**, PhotoEdit/Myrleen Ferguson Cate; **p. 5**, Photolibrary.com; **p. 13**, Photolibrary.com/Banana Stock; **p. 5**, Photolibrary.com/Thomas Kremer; **p. 13**, Science Photo Library/Adam Hart-Davis; **p.18**, Science Photo Library/James King-Holmes.

Cover photograph of breakfast cereal reproduced with permission of fotolibrary.com/Foodpix.

The publishers would like to thank Dr Sarah Schenker for her assistance in the preparation of this book.

Disclaimer

Dedicated to the memory of Lucy Owen

Contents

Any words appearing in bold, **like this**, are explained in the Glossary.

What is breakfast?

Every morning when you wake up, your body needs healthy food. From dinner until morning is the longest time each day that you don't eat. This is called a **fast**. Your morning meal 'breaks' this 'fast', so it is called breakfast.

Breakfast is an important meal. Breakfast gives your body its first **energy** and **nutrition** of the day.

Did your breakfast include any foods from this picture?

Muesli and milk, a banana, and a glass of tomato juice are a good breakfast in the United States.

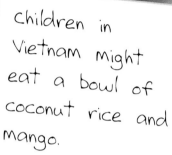

Children in Vietnam might eat a bowl of coconut rice and mango.

In Mexico a favourite breakfast is a wrap made with scrambled eggs, vegetables, and soured cream.

In France, many people like a croissant and hot chocolate for breakfast.

Why do you eat breakfast?

Healthy breakfast foods give **energy** to your body. You use this energy to move about when you play or work. Even sitting still, you need energy to think and learn. The energy in food is called **kilojoules** or calories, and all foods have different amounts.

food	kilojoules	(calories)
two slices of wholemeal toast	661	(158)
two hard-boiled eggs	615	(147)
banana	418	(100)
glass of semi-skimmed milk	384	(92)

This table shows some breakfast foods and the amount of kilojoules (kJ) they have.

You can see that each food gives your body different amounts of energy. You are using energy from your food all the time.

This bar chart is a guide to the energy a child may use during these activities.

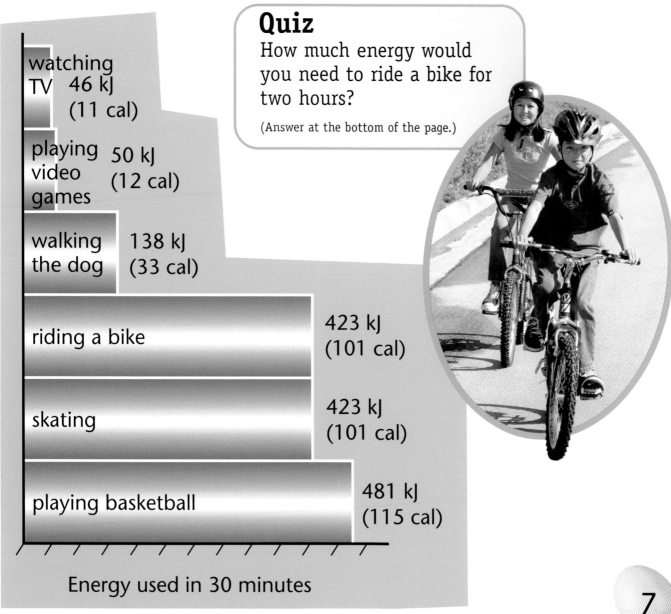

watching TV 46 kJ (11 cal)

playing video games 50 kJ (12 cal)

walking the dog 138 kJ (33 cal)

riding a bike 423 kJ (101 cal)

skating 423 kJ (101 cal)

playing basketball 481 kJ (115 cal)

Energy used in 30 minutes

Quiz

How much energy would you need to ride a bike for two hours?

(Answer at the bottom of the page.)

Answer: You need 1692 kJ (404 cal) to ride a bike for two hours.

What are the healthiest breakfast foods?

The types of food and how much you eat each day is called your **diet**. If you choose foods with good **nutrition**, you will grow well and be healthy. A healthy diet must include many different foods. Foods can be divided into five groups.

The food groups needed for a healthy diet are shown in this chart.

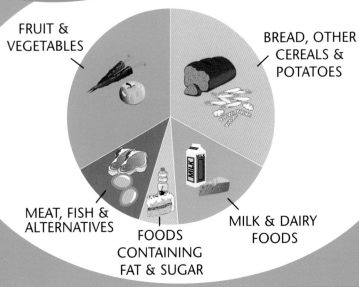

FRUIT & VEGETABLES

BREAD, OTHER CEREALS & POTATOES

MEAT, FISH & ALTERNATIVES

FOODS CONTAINING FAT & SUGAR

MILK & DAIRY FOODS

The chart above shows that some food groups should make up a smaller amount of your daily diet. If you use this chart, you can make sure that you get the food balance right.

Good breakfast foods from the "bread, other cereals, and potatoes" group include wholemeal toast and porridge. Many children eat fruit in the morning, such as strawberries and melon. You could have some yoghurt or a glass of milk from the "milk and dairy foods" group.

Eggs are included in the "meat, fish, and alternatives" group. Vegetables, such as grilled tomato or mushrooms, are great for breakfast.

These foods contain all the fat and sugar you need.

This breakfast includes something from each food group.

Breakfast foods and nutrition

Food provides **nutrients** that your body needs to be healthy. The most important nutrients are water, **carbohydrates, proteins, fats, vitamins,** and **minerals**.

Carbohydrates give you energy. Proteins help your body build new **cells** to grow and repair injuries. Fats provide energy and help your body use vitamins.

Which foods give you these nutrients?

Carbohydrates	Proteins	Fats

wholegrain bagel	eggs	butter
muesli	ham	sunflower oil
wholemeal toast	nuts	cream cheese

Vitamins keep your **immune system** strong. Your immune system fights **germs** to help you stay healthy. It also helps your body heal from injuries. Eating fresh fruit and vegetables is the best way to get the vitamins you need.

Minerals are just as important as vitamins. Calcium is a mineral that you need for strong bones and teeth. Milk, nuts, and meat are breakfast foods that are full of calcium.

Plants combine water, energy from the sun, gases from the air, and minerals from the soil. The food they make is filled with nutrients.

vitamin C
vitamin B
potassium

Vitamins and minerals needed for a healthy body

Vitamins: *A, B, C, D, E, and K*
Minerals: *calcium, potassium, iron, magnesium, phosphorus, and zinc*

minerals
water

Bread, other cereals, and potatoes

An important food group is the "bread, other cereals, and potatoes" group. You should eat foods from this group every day for a healthy **diet**.

These foods are the best source of **carbohydrates** to give your body **energy**. Foods in this group also contain **vitamins**, **minerals**, and **fibre**. Fibre helps keep your **gut** healthy.

These are healthy grain foods made from different cereals.

Breakfast around the world

In China, many children eat a bowl of brown rice and vegetables for breakfast. Brown rice has more nutrients than white rice, and four times the fibre.

Some foods made with cereal grains are better for you than others. All grains come from plants, but they can be whole or refined. Whole grains contain all of their natural nutrients. Refined grains have had some of their nutrients, like fibre, removed.

Wheat, corn, oats, and rice are some grains people eat for breakfast. They are made into foods like bread, breakfast cereal, and pancakes. Always try to choose foods made with whole grains.

Wholemeal bread or toast is a healthy breakfast food. It contains the natural nutrients from the wheat grain.

Fruit and vegetables for breakfast

5-A-DAY
Eat at least 5 portions of fruit and vegetables each day

Fruit and vegetables are very important for good health. They are full of **vitamins**, **minerals**, and other **nutrients**. Fruit and vegetables are high in **fibre** and low in **fat**.

High fibre foods give you **energy** for a longer time. They make you feel full, so you won't be hungry again until lunchtime. Eating fruit and vegetables each day helps keep every part of your body strong and healthy.

You can fill a tortilla with all sorts of tasty vegetables, like peppers, tomatoes, and onions.

At breakfast, vegetables can give meat or egg dishes more colour, flavour and **nutrition**.

Omelette with vegetables

Always ask an adult to help you in the kitchen.

Ingredients:
butter
2 beaten eggs
4 cherry tomatoes
sliced mushrooms
chopped green pepper
grated cheese

Directions:
1. Place a knob of butter in a frying pan on medium heat.
2. Cook the vegetables until tender.
3. Add the egg, then cheese.
4. When the eggs are cooked, serve on a plate with the tomatoes.

More fruit and vegetables!

Fruit and vegetables contain many **vitamins** and **minerals** you need for good health. They are also high in **fibre** and low in fat. Eating fruit is the best way to get vitamin C, which helps prevent illness. There are lots of tasty fruits to choose from at breakfast.

These are just a few of the fruits you could choose at breakfast.

Farmers around the world grow apples, bananas, melons, peaches, berries, and other fruits that people like to eat. The fruit travels on ships and aeroplanes to markets in every country. That means that even when there is no fruit growing at home, you can eat fruit from other places.

When fruit is not available fresh, you can buy it frozen or canned. The **nutrients** are almost the same in all fresh and frozen fruits. However, peeled fruit in cans has less fibre. Some canned fruit has added sugar, some is canned in its own juice.

This fruit is packed carefully so that it is kept fresh on the ship.

Healthy milk and dairy foods for breakfast

The "milk and dairy foods" group includes milk and foods made from milk, like cheese and yoghurt. This group provides you with **protein**, **vitamins**, and **minerals**. Calcium is an important mineral found in dairy foods. You need calcium for strong bones and teeth.

Dairy foods low in **fat** are the healthiest choices.

Compare the nutrients of whole and semi-skimmed milk

	kilojoules (calories)	protein	carbohydrates	fats	calcium
whole milk (200 ml)	586 (140)	6.6 g	9.4 g	7.8 g	0.3 g
semi-skimmed milk (200 ml)	401 (96)	6.6 g	10 g	3.2 g	0.3 g

g = grams   ml = millilitres

Plain low fat yoghurt is a healthy food in the "milk and dairy foods" group. It is one of the foods made from milk, and is full of **nutrients**. Yoghurt can be eaten by itself or mixed with other healthy breakfast foods.

Fruit, yoghurt and muesli breakfast layers

Always ask an adult to help you in the kitchen.

tbsp = tablespoons

Ingredients:
   your favourite muesli
   low fat natural yoghurt
   chopped fresh fruit
   chopped walnuts

Directions:
1. Layer 2 tbsp of muesli, 2 tbsp yoghurt, and 2 tbsp of chopped fruit into a tall water or sundae glass.
2. Repeat the layers until the glass is filled.
3. Sprinkle chopped walnuts on top.

Enjoy your healthy breakfast of cereal, dairy, fruit, and nuts.

Meat, fish, and alternatives for breakfast

Eggscellent eggs!

One chicken egg has the highest amount of protein for a food of its size and weight. It also contains 12 vitamins, many minerals and only 5 grams of fat.

Foods in the "meat, fish, and alternatives" group supply your body with **protein**, **minerals**, and **fat**.

You need smaller amounts of the foods in this group, but make sure you have a variety of them in your diet.

Breakfast around the world

In Ethiopia, a favourite breakfast food is eggs – ostrich eggs. One huge egg can feed a whole family. An ostrich egg is ten times larger than a chicken egg and weighs up to 1.4 kilograms.

Foods in the "meat, fish, and alternatives" group include nuts, seeds, and beans. They are all high in **fibre**. Beans are low in fat. Nuts and seeds contain a healthy type of fat.

smoked salmon

grilled bacon

Try something new!
To add variety to your breakfasts, select a different food from the "meat, fish, and alternatives" group each week.

What to drink with breakfast

Water is essential for life. Your body is mostly made of water. Water controls your **temperature**, keeps your skin healthy, and makes joints and muscles move easily. Water carries **nutrients** to all parts of your body and helps get rid of waste. All drinks, like milk and juice, contain water, and are good choices for breakfast.

Just juice, please

Most fruits can be made into delicious juices. The healthiest choices are those that are just juice, with no added sugar.

A great way to drink many nutrients at once is with a breakfast drink. They are healthy, tasty, and fun to make.

For each drink below, place the ingredients into a blender, mix until smooth, and pour into a glass.

Va-va-voom breakfast drink

Always ask an adult to help you in the kitchen.

g = grams   ml = millilitres
tbsp = tablespoons

Ingredients:
   100 ml orange juice
   1 chopped pear or peach
   1 frozen banana (peel before freezing)
   75 g plain low fat yoghurt
   3 tbsp smooth peanut butter

Ready-to-go breakfast drink

Always ask an adult to help you in the kitchen.

g = grams   ml = millilitres
tbsp = tablespoons

Ingredients:
   1 frozen banana (peel before freezing)
   100 ml apple juice
   3 heaped tbsp porridge oats
   2 tbsp runny honey
   100 g fresh fruit (pineapple, strawberries, or raspberries)

23

Breakfast on the run

Some mornings you might not have time to sit down and eat breakfast at home. Maybe you overslept, or you have to leave early for a school trip.

Even if you need something quick and simple to eat in the car or on the school bus, it can still be healthy.

If you are in a hurry, a banana is a good choice from the "fruit and vegetables" group.

Plan ahead for those rushed mornings by having some of these foods ready. Just make choices from all four columns in this chart to make sure you get a good start to the day.

Bread, other cereals, and potatoes	Fruit and vegetables	Milk and dairy foods	Meat, fish, and alternatives
muesli bar	fruit juice	milk	hard-boiled eggs
bagel	apple/banana	yoghurt	almonds
rice cakes	peach	Cheddar cheese	sunflower seeds
toast	lettuce/tomato	butter	sliced meat
muffin	grapes/cherries	cottage cheese	peanut butter
cereal		cream cheese	tofu

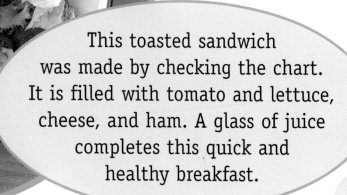

This toasted sandwich was made by checking the chart. It is filled with tomato and lettuce, cheese, and ham. A glass of juice completes this quick and healthy breakfast.

Prepare a safe breakfast

Germs are tiny living creatures too small to see. They make food go off, and they can make you sick.

Wash your hands to clean off germs before you touch food or eat. Make sure **cooking utensils** and kitchen areas are clean.

How to wash your hands

1. *Make suds on your hands with soap and water.*
2. *Rub your hands together as long as it takes to sing the Happy Birthday song.*
3. *Rinse in clean water.*
4. *Repeat steps 1, 2, & 3.*

Wash fresh fruit and vegetables before you use them. If you touch raw meat or eggshells, wash your hands again, as these may have germs on them.

The best way to make food safe is to keep cold foods cold, and hot foods hot. Germs like warm temperatures between 4° C (40° F) and 60° C (140° F). Refrigerators are colder than 4° C to keep food fresh. Cooking food to 82° C (180° F) kills germs.

Look at the label to make sure food isn't too old. Throw food away if it has mould on it or if it looks or smells bad.

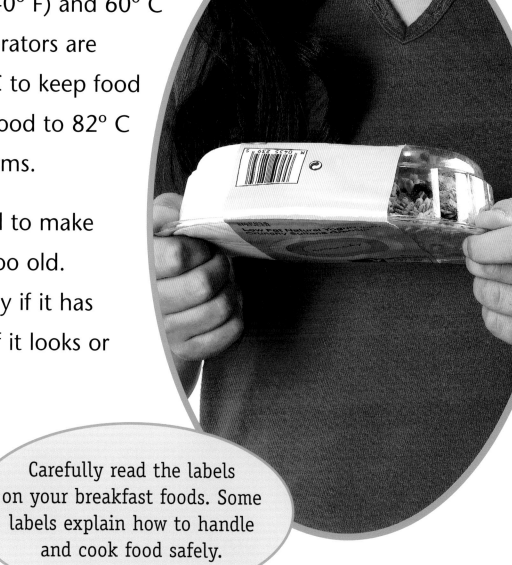

Carefully read the labels on your breakfast foods. Some labels explain how to handle and cook food safely.

Breakfast planner: pancakes and fruit

preparation time: 20 minutes

Always ask an adult to help you in the kitchen.

- Cooking utensils:
  - non-stick frying pan
  - mixing bowl
  - mixing spoon
  - spatula

- Ingredients:
  - 2 tbsp butter
  - pancake mix (try to use wholemeal)
  - eggs
  - milk
  - 200 g chopped fresh fruit or berries
  - 75 g chopped nuts
  - natural yoghurt

g = grams
tbsp = tablespoons

Pancakes are a fun and delicious treat. Here is a recipe for making fruity whole grain pancakes. Enjoy them!

For the best pancakes, always measure carefully and follow the directions on the pancake mix.

Directions:

1. Read the directions on the pancake mix and measure out the ingredients with an adult.
2. Mix the pancake batter until smooth.
3. Ask an adult to preheat the frying pan on medium heat.
4. Melt the butter in the pan.
5. Using a cup, pour the pancake batter into the pan. Make 3-4 thick pancakes, or 1 thin one.
6. Turn the pancakes when they become brown around the edges.
7. Cook for another minute.
8. Place the cooked pancakes on a plate.
9. Top or fill with fruit, nuts, and natural yoghurt.
10. Pour a glass of juice and enjoy your breakfast.

You could make American pancakes like these, or you could roll up your fruit and yoghurt in a thin pancake.

Find out for yourself

Selecting foods for a healthy diet is important, but it doesn't have to be difficult. Learn the basic food groups and how much you need from each one. Make good choices and enjoy good health.

Books to read

Look after yourself: Get Some Exercise!, Angela Royston (Heinemann Library, 2004)

Look after yourself: Eat Healthy Food!, Angela Royston (Heinemann Library, 2004)

Go Facts: Healthy Eating, Paul McEvoy (A & C Black, 2005)

Healthy Body Cookbook: Fun Activities and Delicious Recipes for Kids, Joan D'Amico and Karen Eich Drummond (John Wiley & Sons, 1998)

Using the Internet

Explore the Internet to find out more about healthy breakfast foods. Websites can change so if some of the links below no longer work, don't worry. Use a search engine, such as **www.yahooligans.com** or **www.internet4kids.com** and type in key words such as "breakfast foods," "healthy diet" or "breakfast nutrition".

Websites

www.nutrition.org.uk Click on "Education", then "Cook club" for some great recipe ideas.

www.eatwell.gov.uk There is lots of information about diet and health here, as well as quizzes and games.

www.5aday.nhs.uk Find out easy ways to get your 5-a-day, and some delicious smoothie recipes.

Glossary

carbohydrate   the part of food that gives you energy

cell   the body's smallest building block of living tissue

cooking utensils   the knives, spatulas, and small tools used to prepare food

diet   what you usually eat and drink

energy   the power needed for your body to work and stay alive

fast   to give up eating food for a time

fats   nutrient from food that gives you energy

fibre   material in foods that is not digested but keeps your gut healthy

germ   a tiny living creature that can cause sickness

gut   the parts of your body that your food moves through

kilojoule   a measurement of food energy

mineral   nutrient needed to make the body work correctly

nutrient   substance (such as a vitamin, mineral, or protein) that people need to grow and stay healthy

nutrition   the part of food your body can use

protein   nutrient in food that gives you energy and is used for growth and repair

temperature   how hot or cold something is

vitamin   nutrient in food that the body needs to stay healthy

whole grains   grains that have most of their natural fibre and nutrients

Index

Titles in the *What's On Your Plate?* series include:

Hardback   1 406 20255 X

Hardback   1 406 20256 8

Hardback   1 406 20260 6

Hardback   1 406 20261 4

Find out about the other titles in this series on our website www.raintreepublishers.co.uk